The S

System

Unlock the Strategies of the Ultra Wealthy to Reduce Tax, Accumulate Wealth and Protect Assets

By Bruce Willey, JD, CPA

#1 Bestselling Author

Published by
ATBP Publishing
Cedar Rapids, IA
https://www.americantbp.com/

Copyright 2018 Bruce Willey, American Tax & Business
Planning, LLC
Printed in the United States of America

Table of Contents

FREE TAX SAVINGS ESTIMATE

If you **want to predictably Save On Taxes Each Year**...*Even If You Can't Read A Spreadsheet*, **join me for a free Tax Savings Estimate!**

http://www.americantbp.com/optimizemytaxes

Welcome to The Secret System!

Introduction

Most successful business ecosystems have both a lawyer and an accountant. I've had the pleasure to work with many business owners throughout my 30 years of practice holding both titles. This has given me an invaluable point of view; having both background, I have been able to handle some pretty tough situations for my clients as well as help them become wealthy, or wealthier, by using 'the system' in the right way. Writing this book allows me to share that expertise with you so you can enjoy having more wealth, paying less tax (legally) and protecting your assets.

This book is intended for those business owners throughout the United States who want effective, pragmatic advice to help them maximize the value of their business and personal wealth at each stage of the business lifecycle.

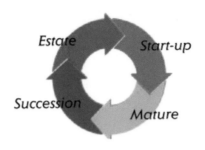

Estate

Start-up

Succession

Mature

These chapters are not intended as a comprehensive planning guide. The principles and strategies discussed have consistently helped business owners grow both their business and their individual wealth, while protecting their property. Some of the techniques or concepts may not be of interest or apply to you, and that's okay. The beauty of working with diverse and successful clients is helping them consider all options to create the best plan for them.

This book wasn't written to be a #1 Bestseller (although that is the case). Instead, my intention was to give you practical information you can use AND start a narrative conversation to get to know each other a bit and, ultimately, help you decide if we will work together at some point.

The goal of this book is three-fold in helping you maximize:
1. Your cash flow and working capital.
2. The value of your business.

3. Your personal wealth at all stages of the business lifecycle.

This book matches my style – it's concise but packed with information you can use. I want to show you the inside secrets of how the ultra-wealthy manage their financial strategies so you can reduce tax, accumulate wealth and protect your assets.

I will also share with you some easy-to-use tools to guide your thinking and help set you up for success in managing your wealth more effectively.

To be perfectly transparent, I'm not big on promoting my work because I'm too busy doing it. At the same time, I recognize that you would never get this information if I didn't take the time to share what I know and that's what drives me – knowing there are people like you who could be scammed by the system, robbed of your money or be paying too much because you're following what you think are the rules.

What I'm going to share here is proven through a lot of experience and it's what usually only the ultra-wealthy can access (because they have the cash and motivation to do so). I want to change that. What you're about to learn here

---

works and your financial life will be better if / when you put this information to work as your own personal wealth strategies.

You don't need to be 'ultra-wealthy' yet to get value from this book, by the way. The key is to use these strategies to make the most of what you do have and, over time, you optimize your chances for becoming ultra-wealthy.

If there are two rules to take from reading this book, it would be these:

<u>One</u>: accomplishment of these objectives requires planning and implementation.

<u>Two</u>: you have to document your structures, your transactions and everything else in order for it to work for you as intended.

With that, let's get started – your wealth is on the line.

Happy pursuits.

Bruce Willey

P. S.: If you get value from what you learn in this book, or save taxes or protect your assets, will you please post a short review on Amazon? If you DON'T like it, send me an email, tell me why and I'll give you your money back, ok?

I read all the reviews personally, so I can make this book even better. If you'd like to leave a review, just visit this link: http://bit.ly/TheSecretSystemUnlocked

Endorsements and Accolades

"While paying taxes is the privilege of living in our great country, not implementing the smart tax savings strategies Bruce recommends is just throwing money out the window. Fortunately, I listened, I implemented, and I saved… over 6 figures in my first year of working with Bruce. Many thanks to Bruce and his team." ~ **Chris H., North Carolina**

"Bruce has helped us with our taxes for several years now. He is a true professional and any business owner looking to make sure they are taking advantage of every tax reduction strategy available to them would do well by talking to Bruce and taking his advice." ~ **Matt D., Kentucky**

"After working through the process and implementing the majority, all but one of the suggestions made by Bruce. In less than 2 years, we have saved over $100,000. Another great thing - we will continue to legally save money each year moving forward! We are really okay with that!" ~ **Stephanie F., Arizona**

"I highly recommend Attorney Bruce Willey and his accounting firm. They're very organized, responsive and have great communication skills." ~ **Terry T., Indiana**

"Bruce Willey is the tax planning CPA you always wanted, but you could never seem to find. He has a laser focus in using the tax code to YOUR benefit, and he's not afraid to use creative out of the box thinking to help you reduce your tax liability. He's also an attorney, so he knows what is legal and what is not. He keeps you on the right side of the law, so you don't get in trouble with the IRS. If you don't talk to Bruce, you are missing out." ~ **Mike R., Texas**

"Julia and I are extremely pleased with the responsiveness and quick turnaround from your team. Alexus and Carrie are fantastic and clearly represent your firm very well." ~ **Chris A., Nevada**

"Bruce has given us more of an opportunity to give out and give to the community. We have been blessed to be able to do that working through Bruce. It has been a value added we are extremely happy with his efforts and his performance." ~ **Jack T., Illinois**

Who Am I and Why Should You Trust or Listen to Me?

I remember the day vividly, though it was many years ago, when one of my best clients was in the conference room signing tax returns. He looked at me, and asked, *"Are we doing everything we can do to reduce this tax bill?"*

See he was writing a seven-digit check - and it hurt. I could see the pain in his face. He wanted to make sure that we were doing everything we could to legally minimize the bill.

At the time, I responded with a simple "yes" but, in my heart, I knew the answer was something different. I honestly didn't know - but I resolved then and there to find a better way to help ease this person's pain as well as the pain of the rest of my clients who were successful and also writing big checks.

So I set upon a journey to learn everything I could - to listen to ideas from the best in the country, to combine strategies in a way that would create customizable, cost-effective plans that provided measurable value to my clients. As a result of that journey, I have learned much about my clients, the tax code and myself.

Since that time, I've helped hundreds of business owners reduce their tax bills legally with the average savings being approximately $90,000 a year. Many of my clients realize savings significantly in excess of that amount. This is real money; these are funds that change lives, increase opportunity and help families accomplish their dreams and goals at a much faster pace.

Our planning takes tried-and-true legal strategies and combines them in a way that receives maximum benefits for our clients. We do not rely on any one strategy. The diversification of ideas and concepts provides protection as well as enhances savings opportunities.

I've received phone calls and notes from clients upon selling their business or retiring. Their messages are ones of thanks for helping them realize their goals and dreams at a much quicker pace.

In short, we help you accomplish your dreams and goals at a much quicker pace. It doesn't matter how rich you may be now. Tax savings can be realized. Our most effective planning comes with clients who pay more than $200,000 a year in taxes, but many of our strategies are scalable to benefit people well below that threshold.

Be proud of what you have accomplished and start where you are.

1. General Tax Planning

What do I mean by tax planning? Tax planning is a proactive approach to managing your total income tax burden as guided by a plan, accomplished throughout the year. An effective plan is regular, recurring and scalable based upon the results of the business for any given part of a given year. It always strikes me as odd to see a business owner who has goals, documented in a business plan or similar guiding documents, but typically has no plan with respect to taxes. And, yet, tax is a large percentage of their net income.

While your tax preparer may tell you that you are doing all you can to legally reduce your taxes, chances are pretty good that you are not. Even as the tax law changes over time, planning opportunities always exist.

For instance, I often hear from business owners that their accountant's tax advice was to buy a truck in December to reduce some Section 179 expense and accelerate deductions you would receive over time. Don't get me wrong - it's good advice - BUT it's not really a "plan" unless, of course, the purchase of that truck is vital to the business and it is needed regardless of the tax benefits.

An effective tax plan:

• Examines your business and its key components, including risks.

• Analyzes your major spending areas.

• Takes into account your employees and their demographics.

• Looks at capital and borrowing needs as well as your spending and wealth accumulation needs.

A plan helps construct an essential platform for the business; a properly constructed plan is also scalable as your business grows and changes.

There are many tax preparers in the United States, but there are not nearly as many professionals who are financial planners first. The right professional is required to build a scalable plan and monitor its effectiveness periodically. It's simply not enough to have the plan but you must also consistently measure and evaluate its effectiveness. Planning is not something you do when your year has concluded, or while you are collecting records to prepare your return. It must be done periodically and continually throughout the year.

Example of Effective Tax Rates

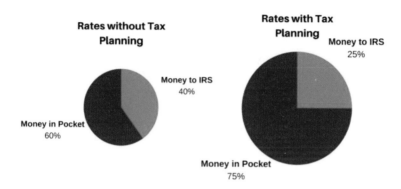

Additionally, tax planning normally entails a combined number of strategies working together, rather than reliance on a singular strategy. One exception to this general rule is use of and ESOP (Employee Stock Ownership Program) but, even in the ESOP setting, other complimentary strategies can be deployed.

What are the advantages of doing a tax plan?

Well, first, the business can realize significant increases in cash flow. That increased cash flow can be used to increase the working capital of the business and allow the business to grow at a faster pace with lower amounts of debt. Additionally, that cash flow can be taken by the owners, hopefully in tax-efficient ways, to grow personal wealth and protect property.

The second advantage of tax planning is that the process allows us to examine your business and make changes, positively influencing the business and finding benefits that previously were unavailable to the business owner. This identification of opportunities allows us to plan more effectively both for now and the future.

The third advantage of an effective tax plan is it will allow your business to grow and to accumulate resources faster, enhancing the value of the business and your wealth accumulation opportunities.

What are the disadvantages of not doing a tax plan?

I sometimes hear from people that they don't want to do tax planning because it's going to raise a red flag and increase their chances of audit. The truth is that no one can speak with certainty as to what causes an audit.

With that in mind, whether you do planning or not, there is a plan in place - why not make it yours? Your audit risk is the same. So long as you are executing legal planning and documenting the strategies, you are prepared to win an audit should one occur. That is why I am a big proponent of proactively creating and following a plan built for you. Do things correctly, enjoy any resulting tax savings and win any audit that may occur.

The second disadvantage of not planning is the very profound risk that a business owner is going to overpay their taxes. By not planning, you are diminishing your cash flow, diminishing your wealth, increasing the risks inherent within a business and, finally, creating a cycle that isn't good for the long-term prospects of the business.

Overpaying your taxes leads to a nagging feeling "there has to be a better way." You owe it to yourself and your family to find a credible tax planner and consider them as a member of your team. The right planner can be invaluable and a key component of your success. Their fees are an investment - not an expense. Overpaying taxes can lead to stress, strain on multiple levels and cause the business to take on too much debt.

I encourage you to ask yourself these questions (and, as my coach Dan Sullivan of the Strategic Coach says, "All progress begins with complete honesty").

1. When is the last time your tax preparer contacted you and provided you with a strategy to legally reduce your

taxes - without you asking?

Having trouble thinking of one?

2. Is the advice you receive always in response to a question that you asked?

3. Is the advice last-minute?

4. Is the guidance a one-off idea or suggestion without any recurring value?

5. Is the idea part of a comprehensive plan?

Your answers to these questions are most likely similar to many business owners – eye-opening and disappointing. Do yourself a favor and invest a little time to find an experienced planner who will help you develop a plan, address the questions above and change the answers.

Is tax planning illegal?

At times, I hear objections about tax planning "being illegal" or "I don't want to go to jail." Well, neither do I!

Tax planning is legal. The courts have consistently held

---

that it's not among the duty of Americans to overpay their income taxes.

"Anyone may so arrange his affairs so that his taxes be as low as possible."
~ Judge Leonard Hand

"In America, there are two tax systems - one for the informed and one for the uninformed. Both are legal."
~ Judge Leonard Hand

"Over and over again courts have said that there is nothing sinister in so arranging one's affairs as to keep taxes as low as possible. Everybody does so, rich or poor; and all do right, for nobody owes any public duty to pay more than the law demands: taxes are enforced exactions, not voluntary contributions. To demand more in the name of morals is mere cant."
~ Judge Leonard Hand

The primary test as to whether a tax plan is legally permissible, or not, is a review of the difference between tax avoidance and tax evasion.

Tax evasion is illegal and could result in jail time, in addition to other penalties. Tax evasion is generally considered an illegal act to escape paying taxes. The illegal acts include deliberate concealment of money, deductions for items not legally allowed or which are fictitious and overstating eligibility for tax credits, exemption or other items allowed by law. The key distinction between evasion and avoidance is that evasion involves an illegal act.

Tax avoidance is the arrangement of your personal and business affairs to legally minimize your tax liability. It means finding strategies and tools to allow reduction of income taxes that might otherwise be due.

Tax planning is tax avoidance, which is the process of using tools and methods which are legal to reduce your income tax burden.

I was at a party once where a representative from a local U.S. Attorney's office was also there. He was a friend and introduced me to a tax person in his office. We talked for a bit about our planning and what we do for clients. At the end of the conversation, he said, "*No tax evasion in what you are doing - sounds like great tax avoidance strategies.*"

As a business owner, you must also understand that tax planning may involve trade-offs - there may be a benefit from use of a strategy, yet a drawback in another area. There could be issues with one strategy that may present an opportunity with another strategy.

We see this often in the qualified retirement planning area. You get an income tax deduction with a 401(k) contribution now but, when you withdraw the money, the money comes out at ordinary income tax rates - including gains. That's a common trade-off that we as planners encounter. Some people like the protection of the 401(k) and utilize it to its maximum. Other people, understanding the trade-off, may choose alternate tools, but this is all part of the process in developing a proper plan and helping you decide what is most appropriate for you.

It's important to note that your plan should not exceed the administrative capabilities of your business. Countless times, I've had clients who would benefit from sophisticated planning techniques. Unfortunately, they simply do not have the administrative capabilities to process the entries and make sure that the transactions are occurring as scheduled, on time and correctly.

For that reason, you must make an honest assessment of your administrative capabilities. And while your planning should utilize all available faculties, it is important not to exceed your ability to execute on those administrative capabilities or, at the very least, be mindful of how to increase capabilities so you can capture an opportunity.

How tax planning is executed

Tax planning is not a magic pill to swallow or an easy button you can press. The process can be streamlined but some work must be done, and you have to be committed to getting results.

There are four primary ways to legally reduce income taxes for business owners.

1. Convert after-tax expenditures to pretax.

I frequently have conversations with business owners along the following line, *"Would you rather use a dollar to buy something or $0.60 to buy that same thing?"*.

Obviously, it's a rhetorical question - the answer is obvious. The power of being able to spend pretax dollars is that your purchasing power is enhanced - a dollar equals a dollar. Utilizing after-tax monies to acquire something means you are only allowing yourself to use $0.60 of that dollar. That means you have to start with two dollars and pay tax to be able to buy that $1 item purchased with pre-tax dollars.

The leveraged effect of using the value of your pretax dollar is potentially the most important tax planning tool we have available to us.

2. Reduce taxable income by using exempt or excluded categories of income.

The tax code has several areas that allow you to legally exclude income from an income tax return. An effective tax plan maximizes these categories with respect to your particular business operations.

For instance, did you know that your business could rent outside space for a business purpose? Did you know that space could be your home? Now, you might be asking 'why is this important? The answer is that it is simply one way that income can fall into a tax-excludable category. Income that comes from renting your home for fourteen or less days per year is EXEMPT from income tax.

3. Defer the tax that is paid on certain items occurring in your business.

If we can't legally avoid income tax, then the next best thing is to defer. Occasionally, I'll have a conversation with someone who says:

"I don't like deferral techniques because it just leads me down the road to the unknown and the income tax could be greater later. So, I should just do it now."

It's hard to challenge that kind of statement, except to state that the longer you can keep the full value of your dollar, the better off you typically are because future law is unknown - particularly in this age of expiring provisions and retroactive changes to laws.

For instance, if we put a structure in place that allows you to reduce taxable income by $100,000 this year - a year when you are in the highest tax bracket - you are saving approximately 40% of tax on that deduction. When you later claim the income, say in retirement, you may only be paying tax around 25%. That's a fifteen percent reduction and you had use of your full dollar during that time.

None of us know for certain what's going to happen tomorrow... all we can do is maximize your plan for what we know right now.

"Keep your $ Longer"

4. Leverage income tax rates and benefit differentials that exist between different entity types.

This opportunity to leverage rates exists between companies and individuals, between characterization of ordinary and capital items, and with tax treatment of companies. This category often involves realizing smaller reductions in taxes. It recognizes that a 5%, 10% or 15% reduction for an item is the best we can do so we take it.

The cumulative leverage from these smaller victories can be significant and it is the primary reason I believe planning is a combination of multiple strategies, each yielding benefit which can become substantial in one year and, particularly, over time.

For instance, the top marginal individuals' rate approaches 40%; in certain companies, it is almost half that.

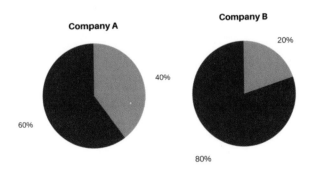

Within these four categories, there are many opportunities to save income taxes. Let me caution you to not rely on any one particular strategy. A tax plan that blends these strategies is more powerful, in my experience, than a plan based on only one - particularly if that strategy is legally precarious.

With any tax plan then, we recommend: using multiple strategies, document them all and, most importantly, don't be greedy with respect to any one strategy.

*****

Key Takeaways

• Tax planning is a proactive approach to managing your total income tax burden as guided by a plan, accomplished throughout the year.

• A plan helps construct an essential platform for the business; a properly constructed plan is also scalable as your business grows and changes.

• There are three benefits to tax planning: 1) realize significant increases in cash flow, 2) consistently identify new opportunities and 3) enable accumulation of wealth faster.

• There is a tax plan in place - why not make it yours instead of the system's?

• Your tax planner should be proactively recommending strategies to save taxes throughout the year.

• The primary test as to whether a tax plan is legally permissible, or not, is a review of the difference between tax avoidance and tax evasion.

• Your tax plan should not exceed the administrative capabilities of your business to see it through operationally.

• There are four primary ways to legally reduce income taxes for business owners.

• The longer you can keep the full value of your dollar, the better off you typically are in any case.

• A tax plan that blends strategies, and documents them, is generally more powerful than relying on a single strategy.

Note: If you're impatient to get started, visit
http://www.americantbp.com/optimizemytaxes for a
complimentary tax savings estimate.

2. Tax Planning: Rules

Before venturing further into the area of tax planning, it is imperative to lay out the foundation from which I approach tax planning. These seven principles are simple, yet profound. They have provided me with useful benchmarks for planning considerations throughout the years and in a myriad of planning situations. These fundamentals can be broken down as follows.

1. Never spend a dollar to save $0.40 of tax.

Let's return to our example of a tax advisor advising a client to purchase a truck at the end of the year. This strategy takes advantage of certain accelerated depreciation benefits of acquiring a vehicle that weighs over 6,000 pounds. I always counter this with the question: *Did you need the truck?*

Because if you don't need the truck, you have spent a bunch of money to save roughly $0.40 of each dollar. Most people like shiny new things, so this advice makes one happy through instant gratification, but it is not a smart way to spend your money.

From my planning perspective, we have to continue our search for additional ways to reduce taxes beyond buying the truck. If there isn't a compelling business need, then I don't agree with the adage that you spend the dollar to merely reduce your tax bill. The planning process and goal for your business should be to make good decisions - not just reduce taxes by spending money unnecessarily.

2. Never turn down a dollar to save $0.40 of tax.

I am continually amazed at the times that clients will do whatever they can to receive cash and, yet, reduce the income they claim in a given year.

Reasonable deferrals of income, which does not place tax income in jeopardy, can be attained and can be a part of an effective tax plan. Simply putting checks in a drawer until next year is not an effective plan.

Too often, I've seen clients turn down non-repeatable business and lose an opportunity by being shortsighted in this regard. You are still ahead even after paying the tax, which is an important concept to remember. Sometimes the best planning is to pay the tax.

3. Whether you realize it or not, you have a plan - the question is whether it is yours or not.

Their Plan

This concept is straightforward and used in a number of different contexts in society today. However, it is completely true, particularly with respect to your business and tax matters.

If you do not take the time to work on your business, to develop a plan and establish measurable thresholds, then your business may suffer in multiple ways.

More importantly, however, if you don't proactively plan and something unexpected or tragic were to happen to you or your business, then the rules of society - your particular state's and federal law - will control the outcome of your business as well as family decisions.

So I implore you to - regardless of whatever your plan is and the qualified professional you choose to work with – live by your plan and not someone else's.

4. Document, document, document.

An audit by the Internal Revenue Service (IRS), Department of Labor, workforce development or anything similar by any federal, state, county or city governmental agency is absolutely no fun whatsoever.

No one reliably knows what causes an audit. Most people, upon receiving a letter from the governmental agency, immediately have a headache, stomach ache and cold sweat pouring down their face. This is inevitable.

The only proactive step to offer someone going through this painful, and potentially lengthy, process is to prepare to win the audit if it should ever occur. The only way to do that is to have a plan, execute it and then document what you do.

Understand that excellent documentation doesn't mean an audit won't occur. The audit may occur anyway.

Additionally, once in an audit, there may always be a disagreement with the IRS or state tax authorities about a particular position taken on a tax return with respect to an item or series of transactions. Without documentation, you lose.

With documentation, you can win the audit or at least improve your ability to negotiate an acceptable outcome. Frequently, even though I believe you can win a position, a client may choose to settle so they can end the audit - it's always your choice.

In any case, I can't emphasize this enough - document, document, document. In the absence of documentation, you will lose nearly every time.

Documentation is the only way to win. Do it when an event occurs and you will be as well-prepared as you can be to WIN.

5. Don't shop for the cheapest provider - look for the best.

People don't brag about seeing the cheapest doctor in town – they brag about working with the best. The same goes for your financial providers.

Your tax plan is an investment, not a cost. Personally, I strive to provide measurable results to clients. This concept is sometimes a little bit difficult to understand, but proper tax planning should yield a return that outweighs the cost of the plan.

Let's take the tax return preparation business, for instance. That business, due to improvements in technology and rules promulgated by the IRS, has become much more of a commoditized business in the last few years. Literally, the software does the thinking for a lot of preparers. And, candidly, that may be fine for the tax returns of half of America.

The wise business owner, however, finds the best tax planning person and utilizes a tax preparation service that will find them dollars, maximize the value of various strategies available to the client and become a sounding board for the business owner in various phases of the business. If the members of your team aren't presently performing at a level that you expect of them, keep looking because they're not the right teammate for you and your business. Ask yourself whether you prefer cheaper services now (and potentially overpaying) OR if it's worth it to you to pay more (and save more).

Besides, have you ever stopped to consider why a provider might be the lowest-cost provider in town? There's usually a reason.

To summarize:

It baffles me that taxes can represent nearly half of a business's net income while very little planning to legally reduce taxes is undertaken. A plan following these simple rules can yield significant, measurable and legal reduction in income tax.

The sooner the business owner understands that "tax is art", the sooner they can identify ways to legally reduce income taxes. And the sooner the company can be leveraged into a higher growth pattern.

Don't look at your tax return preparation as an expense. Don't look at your tax planning as an expense either. Instead, consider tax planning and tax return preparation as an investment, and measure the dollars saved in the return to understand your benefit.

6. The amount of your refund does not matter.

To IRS   **From IRS**

The objective of tax planning for business owners should be to pay the lowest amount of tax legally possible. How you choose to finance the taxes to be paid - by either a refund or by owing – is basically irrelevant from a tax planning perspective.

Far too much attention is spent these days on the amount of a refund. Success or failure of the tax process is often dictated by whether a refund is received and the amount of the refund.

A person could be over-paying their taxes by $1,000, still obtain a refund and yet they are satisfied with the refund – because they don't know what they don't know. They have no idea that they overpaid their taxes. Spending time with planners and preparers who understand the opportunities to help you pay the lowest tax possible is the proper course of action.

It's important to point out that you can give the same tax information to 10 different tax preparers and end up, in most cases, with 10 completely different tax returns being prepared. A lot of subjectivity is utilized by the tax preparer and their presentation of your materials, and that presentation can have a profound effect on the bottom-line income tax amount owed by you and your company.

7. Finally, I implore you - the business owner - to ask questions.

If you walk out of your preparer's office with questions that are unanswered… well, shame on you.

You owe it to yourself to understand what is going on with your tax return and why. You sign it stating everything is accurate and if you haven't reviewed it, your signature is under a penalty of perjury. Shouldn't you read it and understand it?

At the time you pick up your tax return, it may not matter for whatever reason – you might be in a hurry or running late for something else. I understand that but, to not review your return, and to not compare it to your books and records, is potentially a big mistake.

So ask questions. It's crucial you understand these key components of your business and look at the materials not only for the short-term but also for a long-term perspective, so you can maximize the value of your business.

*****

Key Takeaways

• Never spend a dollar to save $0.40 of tax.

• Never turn down a dollar to save $0.40 of tax.

• Whether you realize it or not, you have a plan - the question is whether it is yours or not.

• Document, document, document.

• Don't shop for the cheapest provider - look for the best.

• The amount of your refund does not matter.

• Ask questions and understand the answers! Oh - and ask more questions.

Bonus

Free Tax Savings Estimate!

Visit

http://www.americantbp.com/optimizemytaxes

to see if you're qualified.

3. Tax Planning: Tools

We strongly recommend that you retain qualified professionals to assist with considerations, adoptions, tax planning or reduction execution of any strategies.

So, what are some of the tools that may be available to you as a business owner? Remember, documentation of both the adoption and utilization of all strategies is incredibly important to the success of any tax plan.

The first "tool" we generally consider is structural. Is your business in the correct entity type? Does your business and its parts justify more than one entity? Most companies have many different parts, with many streams of income. Perhaps some different components can be rolled out into separate stand-alone businesses.

There are three basic types of entities - corporations, limited liability companies (LLC) and partnerships. Each one of those entity types can have a number of different tax opportunities, so actually considering options before setting up the company is incredibly important. I always try to make business considerations come first while evaluating the administrative capabilities of my client's team.

Corporations are prevalent in society and have a lengthy history in statute and case law. This type of company can elect to pay tax directly (C-Corp) or pass-through the tax effects to its owners (S-Corp). Benefits vary between the companies depending upon the selected tax treatment. For instance, a person who owns more than 2% of an S-Corp is not eligible for certain employee benefits.

Limited liability companies are newer to the entity landscape and are incredibly flexible company types. You can elect the tax treatment of an LLC as either corporate (S or C) or partnership. One owner LLC's are disregarded and can escape the burden of a separate tax return filing.

Again, benefits and rules vary depending upon the choices made.

Partnerships have been around a while as well - their usage has diminished with the rise in LLC's. A drawback to partnerships cured by LLC's is the partnership trait of one partner having to have unlimited liability for obligations of the partnership. This liability exposure can be effectively mitigated with planning, but LLC's are often chosen as an efficient and cost-effective way to solve this issue.

The choice of entity type can also have a profound effect on liability exposure, as we will discuss later in our asset protection materials.

Businesses will often utilize different entity types, with different features and attributes. The blend of structures and attributes can often yield significant benefits BUT be mindful of taxes and trade-offs.

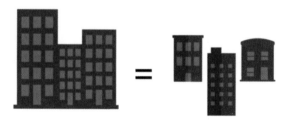

How do you know if your business can be broken into pieces? By looking closely at your business and asking questions.

We identify self-sustaining businesses within your business that will justify separate income streams. Next, we identify the best types of entities available to accomplish your goals and the purpose of your comprehensive tax plan. This is achieved by realizing that some companies have different income tax rates and different timing attributes for recognition of income and expense items.

Once the plan is determined, companies are set up in the appropriate jurisdictions, contracts and ownership issues determined, and then we are ready to use the structures within the context of the plan.

The next "tool" we evaluate involves your children. Your children help with the business one way or another - why not pay them for their services? Services they may provide could be modeling in company advertisements, managing your social media accounts, cleaning the office, filing documents, answering the phone, etc.

Pay your kids a salary and let them pay tax on the earnings. Teach them how to manage money at a young age. Allocate some of their earnings into a Roth IRA which allows withdrawals for education and first-time homebuyer expense.

Why not leverage the resources that are being committed to your business anyway?

A third common, but underutilized, "tool" is qualified retirement plans. Qualified retirement plans can be an incredibly effective way to reduce your income tax.

Different qualified plans have different contribution levels, different company match levels and varying abilities for the company to provide profit-sharing contributions. Most qualified plans come with very few administrative costs, yet businesses often fail to create, offer or fund such plans for their employees or themselves. I hear a number of reasons for not putting a qualified plan in place - cost, administrative burden, and that no one else in the company wants one – but that doesn't mean you cannot establish one for yourself.

Any good tax plan starts with the foundation of a good, qualified plan, as this type of plan not only benefits the owner of the business but can also provide a powerful retention and reward system for employees of the organization.

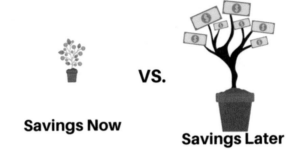

Savings Now   **VS.**   **Savings Later**

Another planning "tool" is nonqualified plans. Nonqualified plans allow the business owner to reward key employees of the organization and exclude others. This can be a particularly powerful type of planning for key employees.

We use these plans quite often when there is significant tax rate leverage between an individual and a company. Nonqualified plans can also be a powerful tool to help a business retain key personnel and also provide value in an exit-planning scenario.

There are many charitable giving "tools" which can substantially reduce taxable income as well. For instance, you can participate in a donor-advised fund which can allow the transfer of appreciated securities to the benefit of charity, without paying tax on gains and getting a deduction for the value of the contribution.

Conservation easements are a variation on charitable "tools" that can be very powerful in reducing income tax as it often provides a multiplier effect on your dollar in deductions. A multiple can often be two to four times your cash contribution. So, if you pay $20,000 for an easement, your charitable deductions could be $40,000 or more. Be careful in this area that reputable valuation professionals are involved in setting values and that the company you are working with has a good reputation and will stand behind their easement if an audit occurs.

The charitably-inclined can also find tax opportunities to help with the sale of the business or succession planning for business owners.

The tools discussed here are a few of the many dozen different ways one can reduce income tax burden, often by merely capturing what a client is already doing but simply labeling it differently or adjusting the behavior to fit a beneficial category.

Remember that, while this book talks about different tools and strategies, you are the lynchpin for your tax planning to be successful. Take it step-by-step, make micro-commitments to yourself to keep going and make the investment of time and resources in the process and working with the professional.

The areas presented for our tax planning tools are broadly based, with many variations and opportunities existing within each group. The wisdom of an experienced planning professional is absolutely essential to proper execution and full realization of planning benefits.

*****

Key Takeaways

• Documentation of both the adoption and utilization of all strategies is incredibly important to the success of any tax plan.

• Exploring the most appropriate business structure is the first tool to reduce tax expense.

• You can pay your children a salary and teach them about finances starting at a young age.

• Qualified retirement plans can be an incredibly effective way to reduce your income tax.

• Nonqualified plans allow the business owner to reward key employees of the organization and exclude others.

• Charitable giving options can substantially reduce taxable income.

• Conservation easements can often provide a multiple on your dollar in deductions.

• The wisdom of an experienced planning professional is essential to proper execution and full realization of tax planning benefits.

A Quick Tax Savings Estimate

To see what that might mean for you, go to this page and enter your income as a general total to see what that might be for you.

Visit

http://www.americantbp.com/optimizemytaxes

to calculate what you could be saving by working with the right tax planning professional starting now.

Ease the burden. Enjoy the freedom.

Bruce Willey Inquiry Form

Fill out this form to stay in touch, schedule a meeting with Bruce to discuss building your wealth, saving tax and protecting your assets.

Your Name: _____

Business Name: _____

Mobile Phone: _____

Direct Email: _____

Website: _____

What do you want to discuss with Bruce?

☐ **Build Wealth:** Strategies to accelerate wealth accumulation.

☐ **Save Tax:** Ways to reduce taxes on wealth, income and assets.

☐ **Protect Assets:** Talk about protecting what I have in assets.

☐ **Business Coaching** with Bruce to Grow My Business

☐ **Have Bruce Speak** at My Next Event

☐ **Hire Bruce as Business Advisor** for My Company

☐ Other: _____

Please Attach Your Business Card to this Form
OR Call (319) 390-5555
OR Email scorum@americantbp.com

4. Tax Planning: Asset Protection

We live in a litigious society where you can be sued for anything – literally - whether you did something or not. I often tell my clients a story about a successful business person who thought his assets were protected.

One day, he was on his way home from work and was involved in an auto accident. Not normally a great situation to be in but he ended up being okay.

Unfortunately, someone in the other vehicle lost her life in the accident. The deceased was a neurosurgeon and made substantial money. The ensuing litigation claims were well in excess of the business man's insurance limits and the litigation process was an incredible burden for the business owner, his business and his family.

You see, he was responsible for everything above the insurance limits. His assets were all titled in his name. His entire net worth was at risk, in addition to the pain and guilt he felt from the accident and knowing he played a role in ending the lady's life.

What is asset protection planning?

Asset protection planning is proactively structuring your affairs so that minimal amounts of property are at risk for claims of unsecured creditors, lawsuits or other claims by third-parties or the government. Asset protection planning uses the law to shield your property from such claims.

In the event something unexpected and potentially tragic occurs, you have the peace of mind of knowing that - even if you made a mistake and are found to be at fault and liable - for most of the dangers, your wealth is protected.

Asset protection done properly is much like tax planning. Find a qualified professional, be completely honest and transparent with them, consider all the options and variables, think it through, then adopt and execute the plan. Be sure to review the plan periodically so it can be adjusted for changes in law or circumstances.

Asset
Protection

We live in a society that seems to thrive on conflict, litigation and placing blame on others for circumstances - many seem to be solely in pursuit of a pot of gold.

Litigation is expensive, stressful, distracting and leads to uncertain and unpredictable outcomes. Arbitration claims, candidly, are not much different than litigation – they are just as costly and as unpredictable.

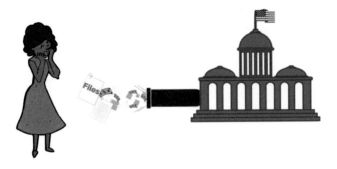

Asset protection can help shortcut some of the downfalls of litigation and arbitration because, if the opposing party knows you have a plan in place, resolution can be accelerated.

Let me stress asset protection is not just for the rich! Asset protection is for anybody with property to lose; arguably, somebody who isn't rich has more to lose than a wealthy person because a claim could be a more significant portion of their wealth.

When is the best time to plan?

The best time to plan is NOW!

Why? Planning *before* a claim arises is the most effective planning and least likely to be set aside by a court.

You see, within the world of asset protection, we are constantly concerned with an area of law called fraudulent transfers or conveyance.

When you execute an asset protection plan, you are often transferring property to entities. Most of the time, that transfer is not executed by paying fair value for the property. That transfer for less than fair value potentially could be set aside by a court as a fraudulent conveyance.

A fraudulent conveyance is a transfer made solely to hinder, delay or defraud a creditor. If the creditor or claim does not exist at the time of the transfer, then your transfer will prevail. When you execute a plan while a claim or lawsuit exists is when you are at greater risk of your planning being set aside.

When you plan, and no claim is present, your concern is limited to statute of limitations issues with respect to the transfer only for any challenge to the planning.

Planning <u>after</u> a claim arises is fraught with peril.

However, planning at any stage is better than no planning at all. For even if a claim exists, you can potentially plan around it by leaving assets available to satisfy the claim if you lose – which means protecting the rest of your assets. We may not be able to protect everything, but we can still protect some assets.

Asset protection can be as simple or complex as you desire. As with tax planning, I prefer to start with basic principles.

<u>The first general rule is that state law often protects certain property from claims.</u>

For example, life insurance, your home and retirement plans are often protected from claims. Learn your state exemptions and then make sure you avoid actions to interfere with the state law exemption.

The second rule is simple - if not protected by state law, consider transferring the asset(s) to a protective entity or trust.

Many different structures can be utilized for their protection of assets, but they are essentially broken down into two categories: entities and trusts.

Though the tools generally break down into two categories, there are a myriad of uses of these tools (and others) to achieve asset protection.

For instance, an "equity strips strategy" approach can further reduce exposure to claims and litigation risk. A typical way of accomplishing an equity strip is to borrow money in the company, reducing the value of any equity available to creditors. Several other varieties of this strategy exist as well.

When we refer to entities, we mean corporations, limited liability companies and partnerships. Each one of these entity types are created pursuant to state law; the requirements for establishment, maintenance and specific provisions vary. When choosing your entity type, it's important to be deliberate and consider the option carefully.

The differences in creditor protection between entity types can be profound; for instance, in most states, a limited liability company has charging order protection (meaning that, in most cases, a creditor cannot take your ownership position but only has a claim to distributed funds or property); corporations do not have this protection.

Trusts also come with a variety of options and differences in the protection provided. One common misconception is if you have a revocable living trust for your assets to avoid probate at the time of death, that this trust also provides asset protection. It does NOT.

To truly protect assets using a trust, you may need to set up a personal residence trust for your home (which may be necessary if your state's homestead exemption is limited) or an asset protection trust. Trusts necessarily involve the trade-off of giving up control of the property versus the asset protection you receive.

Some of the most effective planning is accomplished using entities and trusts together, adding layers of protection at each level of your plan. For instance, we may deploy a holding company Limited Liability Company to own various LLC's, partnerships or C-corporation interests. (Most S-

Corps would terminate their S election if owned by an LLC). In the holding company, the LLC could be owned by another entity or a trust. This arrangement isolates risks into different companies and protects the back-end of the company from claims against the individual.

Asset protection is a necessity for the successful business owner in the present societal environment. The asset protection planning process is much like the tax planning process. Consider your objectives, use more than one strategy, "document, document, document," hire the best professionals you can find to do the job and avoid viewing them as a cost but, instead, as an investment.

Make sure the plan you choose for yourself is cost-effective and that it will work for your business and your family.

Always consider whether the value exceeds the administrative inconvenience and burdens. And, of course, make sure that your planning is current.

*****

Key Takeaways

• We live in a litigious society where you can be sued for anything - literally - whether you did something or not.

• Asset protection planning is proactively structuring your affairs so that minimal amounts of property are at risk for claims of unsecured creditors, lawsuits or other claims by third parties or the government.

• Asset protection can help shortcut some of the downfalls of litigation and arbitration because, if the opposing party knows you have a plan in place, resolution can be accelerated.

• Planning before a claim arises is the most effective planning and least likely to be set aside by a court.

• Asset protection is for anybody with property to lose; arguably, somebody who isn't rich has more to lose than a wealthy person because a claim could be a more significant portion of their wealth.

• Asset protection can be as simple or complex as you desire.

• State law often protects certain property from claims.

• If not protected by state law, consider transferring the asset(s) to a protective entity or trust.

• Asset protection is a necessity for the successful business owner in the present societal environment.

Protect Your Assets

Now is the time to make sure you are protected. Visit:

https://www.americantbp.com/optimizemytaxes

Complete the questionnaire now!

Now is the time to act on what you've already learned.

5. Tax Planning: The Intersection of Tax and Asset Protection Planning

To this point, we have discussed separately how tax and asset protection planning should be accomplished to help attain your business and personal goals. The notion that two comprehensive plans may be necessary, along with the associated costs and time commitments to accomplish them, can be daunting.

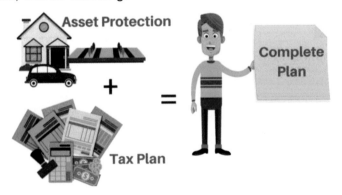

Page:

The good news is that a good tax plan and a good asset protection plan often overlap. Several strategies and planning techniques provide both tax and asset protection benefits. See the following for examples you can consider for your own wealth strategies.

Qualified Plans

A qualified retirement plan can provide significant income deferral opportunities as well as asset protection because most states exempt these types of assets from the claims of creditors. Using defined benefit cash balance 401(k) plans, you can often put away $100,000 or more a year into the plan. This can significantly reduce income tax as well.

Use of Leasing Companies

A business with significant assets may set up a separate leasing company and transfer assets to the leasing company at fair market value, then lease them back. This transaction can result in tax benefits from increased depreciation deduction, and also asset protection as the plan effectively strips assets from the primary business.

Intellectual Property Rights

Intangible property can often have significant independent value and transferring that property to another company can create an income stream which could be tax-advantaged. The transfer of property out of the company also serves as an equity strip for the primary operating business.

Separate Rental Real Estate into Limited Liability Companies

By transferring real estate out of the primary operating business and into separate limited liability companies, we can maintain depreciation deductions yet set up favorable tax conditions for a subsequent sale or transfer. This strategy also serves our asset protection plan by diminishing valuable assets inside of the operating company and reducing the equity a creditor realizes as available to satisfy its claim.

Use of Private Self-Insurance

A business owner may determine, with appropriate professional assistance, that the business does not presently have sufficient insurance to cover the myriad of risks it confronts on a day-to-day basis. The business owner could decide to use private insurance to insure these uncovered risks.

The premium paid by the operating company is deductible and the premium dollars become insurance reserves to the insurance company to cover claims that may be filed. The premium deduction yields immediate tax savings, and the asset protection is two-fold; one, the business is now insured for risks not covered previously, and two, the insurance company itself is equity stripped by reserves set aside pursuant to insurance laws, for claims that may be filed.

Use of Multiple Entities

The use of several entities by a business can often separate risky assets, income streams and other valuable property. By effectively planning ownership of each entity, asset protection can be obtained at many different levels of the enterprise. Additionally, combination of different types of entities for tax purposes can yield income tax savings opportunities.

These examples are just some of the possibilities where the creative use of both techniques and strategies can yield tremendous benefit to the business owner in both areas of concern - tax savings and asset protection.

*****

Key Takeaways

• A good tax plan and a good asset protection plan often overlap.

• A qualified retirement plan can provide significant income deferral opportunities as well as asset protection.

• A business with significant assets may set up a separate leasing company and transfer assets to the leasing company at fair market value, then lease them back.

• Intangible property can often have significant independent value and transferring that property to another company can create an income stream which could be tax-advantaged.

• Separating rental real estate into an LLC can maintain depreciation deductions yet set up favorable tax conditions for a subsequent sale or transfer.

• Use private self-insurance to cover the myriad of risks it confronts on a day-to-day basis as well as for asset protection.

6. What I Do to Help

For more than 30 years, I have worked with business owners and entrepreneurs to lower their tax burdens and protect and maximize their wealth. Helping successful people keep more of what they earned has become a passion of mine.

Though formally trained as a lawyer and CPA, I am an entrepreneur at heart. I seek to make those I work with successful. I am blessed to work with incredibly smart and successful people.

I first started real tax planning 15 years ago when a chance meeting with a client of mine reinforced how significantly taxes could impact even successful businesses. Over time, I listened and learned, read and studied and put together comprehensive plans to help reduce burdens and protect head-earned wealth.

Taking these items to market for clients and prospective clients, I was surprised at how many people didn't know you could do something to legally reduce taxes. I realized then how much help I could be to so many.

To this day, I have worked with hundreds of business owners to help save many thousands of dollars in taxes, every year. We specifically develop plans tailored to each business and owner's needs. We generally start with tax planning as those tax savings can be used to generate wealth and serve as a basis for additional asset protection planning.

To help promote the planning possibilities, I formed American Tax Law Planning in 2012 with a partner.

Recently, it became American Tax & Business Planning, which highlights the broader planning capabilities our team has developed.

Ease the burden. Enjoy the freedom.

Our planning is scalable and suitable for all stages of the business lifecycle. American Tax & Business Planning can provide a comprehensive plan for your business.

I personally strive to design proactive and comprehensive business tax reductions strategies, asset protection and succession planning strategies for our business clients and their owners. The strategies can dramatically and permanently reduce taxes, enhance business capital and allow faster wealth accumulation. Following your plan allows recurring and cumulative savings results which can be realized year after year.

As I am introducing new strategies and concepts to business owners, it can be a challenge to keep up with recurring changes and maintenance. To help our clients cost-effectively maintain and adjust their plans, we created the Compass Master Planning Program – essentially, a maintenance solution to supplement the value of the initial plan.

Master Planning™ Program

The Compass Master Planning Program provides a comprehensive, full service tax strategy and wealth accumulation program that will keep your business on course for success.

There are many aspects within the Compass Master Planning Program to assist with challenges or questions regarding your tax plan. Those categories included are:

• Course Plotting Consultation
  - Personal strategy reviews and strategic counseling on a one-on-one basis with your ATBP Compass Guide each quarter.

• Strategic Information
  - Updates and explanation of current trends in audits as well as information to give you a better view of potential obstacles and opportunities.

• Implementation Guides for Growth
  - Planning and transactions guides as well as legacy planning and tactics to keep your strategies moving in the right direction.

The Compass Master Planning Program is designed to be a more hands-on approach for those clients who don't have the time or capabilities to keep up with the needs of their plan.

We help our clients look ahead for the next 10-15 years. As they are approaching their time to sell or retire, we can provide the tools and support to make that transition as smooth and seamless as possible.

After following their comprehensive plan, the exit process is much simpler. Exit Planning is the final step in the business lifecycle. I am never happier than when - at the end of this cycle - my client has become a friend.

How to Use the Same Strategies as the Ultra-Wealthy to Build, Keep and Protect Their Wealth and Assets

Knowledge is Power

If YOU want to save taxes and attract, build and accelerate your wealth, as well as protect your assets, then you need to know what you don't know.

Submit your information and see what savings you qualify for:

https://www.americantbp.com/optimizemytaxes

Page:

Conclusion

Conclusion

The title of this book – the "Secret System" – was deliberately chosen to grab your attention.

The "secret" may not be obvious to you yet because it is simple and straightforward.

Here it is:

The 'secret' system of the ultra-wealthy and truly successful business owner is the awareness that there are better ways to attain their goals and objectives. They make the time to plan and implement, and they invest in their knowledge and professional team, so that they can realize their objectives sooner.

I have clients who stretch the extremes of success. My most successful clients take the time to work on their business (not just 'in' their business), take chips off the

---

table when appropriate and follow-through on their planning.

A few final thoughts to summarize how simple your plans can be and help you overcome any obstacles you construct to resist proceeding with the realization of increased cash flow and wealth via tax planning <u>and</u> to sleeping better at night by minimizing your risk of loss through asset protection planning.

• Spend the time to find the right advisor.

• Remember the costs are an investment and recoverable over time; such fees should not be viewed as an expense.

• Create a plan that makes sense for you and implement it - NOW!

• Document what you do.

• Be deliberate and considerate in following the plan.

• Enjoy your success.

"You Get to Have Your Wealthiest Life in Every Way"

Ok, I couldn't stop there… because too often I've seen people learn something and not act on it, overpay their taxes because they didn't know what they didn't know, lose their businesses because they didn't protect them properly and, frankly, THIS is what causes me to lose sleep!

My goal for you in this chapter is to motivate and inspire you to act based on what you just read. Whether you work with me or not, find a qualified professional to advise you starting TODAY.

After working with hundreds of business owners, saving them hundreds of thousands of dollars in taxes, helping them accumulate and protect their wealth and assets through strategic tax and asset planning, I know that what you just learned in this short book has the potential of affecting your future in a positive way.

I know it's not easy to get motivated to be 'real' with your numbers, to wish you had more to start with, to clean up the loose ends and wear your big boy / big girl pants around your wealth potential and practices. I get it.

At the same time, if you don't, you put your future (and your family's) at risk.

Why give the tax collectors more than what you should? Why delay the accumulation of real wealth? Why jeopardize your hard-earned assets over some out-of-the-blue litigation? Especially when you don't have to – now you have an idea of what's possible with quality tax and asset planning!

The sooner you take action, the sooner you stabilize your future. If all you did was find a qualified tax and asset planning professional (hello!!!) and book an appointment, you would set a new course in motion that could change everything in your future.

Please – take action now. The day of an accident is not the day to begin. The day you have to file taxes is not the only day to think about them. I'm trying to impress upon you how important it is to get motivated and get moving NOW - - and it begins with finding a qualified professional you can trust to advise you consistently, expertly and with your goals in mind.

In closing - I encourage you to drop me a message at scorum@americantbp.com or visit my website at http://www.americantbp.com/. Take advantage of the tools in this book, let me know your questions and we'll get started changing your future today.

As I said in the beginning of this book, "All progress begins with complete honesty" – you can trust me to tell you what you need to know. How do you know that? Because I made a healthy start in this book you have in your hand right now.

Consider this is your invitation – take what you've learned and use it to upgrade your wealth strategies. And keep me posted on your progress!

Bruce

About Bruce Willey

Bruce Willey JD, CPA, has
served as an accountant, tax
and wealth-building specialist
for individuals and business
owners for over three
decades. As the founder of
American Tax & Business
Planning, LLC, Bruce is also
a bestselling author, sought-
after speaker and an
influential strategist for tax
and business matters.

Bruce prides himself on listening to his clients' needs and
forming strong relationships throughout the planning
process; his specialties include tax minimization,
comprehensive and ongoing wealth and tax guidance as
well as exit planning and transition management for
individuals and business owners.

To accomplish the planning objectives, Bruce and his team
take the time to thoroughly understanding each client's
business as well as their needs and objectives. With this
foundation properly established a comprehensive goal
fulfilling plan is constructed and implemented.

Bruce earned his early professional experience in planning while serving as a tax accountant in Iowa and Colorado. Returning to law school after those stints, he enhanced his planning and strategic thinking capabilities. In 1996, Bruce established his first independent corporation and turned his focus to tax and business law, while also offering accounting and tax compliant services.

In 2012, Bruce formed American Tax and Business Planning and began serving clients as a consultant and tax strategist. Bruce and his team have saved their clients millions of dollars in unnecessary taxes and costs. In addition to the tax savings, clients realize the benefit of a properly structured business enterprise, successful management of inherent business risks and increased security and wealth accumulation for their families.

Bruce received his BBA in accounting from the University of Iowa in 1985. In 1990, he earned a juris doctor with distinction at the same school. Bruce completed Iowa's law program in two years.

He is an active member of AICPA, American Academy of Attorneys – CPA's and several entrepreneur organizations. Bruce regularly attends events as an exhibitor and guest speaker. He showcases his passion for helping successful clients as well as catching up with his current clients.

Outside the office, Bruce enjoys sports. Growing up, Bruce participated in many sports, but his favorites were wrestling and football. While attending the University of Iowa, he was a walk-on football player for Hayden Fry's Iowa Hawkeyes. He also earned his Eagle Scout in the early 1980's. If you get the chance, ask him about how he dropped 43lbs in three weeks for wrestling - if that doesn't show his kind of commitment, what does?

Bruce is a very active parent in his children's high school -- particularly with their chosen sports. He is also very passionate about, of course, any and all University of Iowa sports! He lives with his wife and two children in Iowa.

He can be reached at his LinkedIn page:

https://www.linkedin.com/in/bruce-willey-b574b14/

Also, follow ATBP on Facebook:

https://www.facebook.com/Americantaxandbusinessplanning/

Book Bruce Willey to Speak

Book Bruce Willey as your Keynote Speaker and You're Guaranteed to Learn Ways to Accelerate Your Wealth, Keep More of What You Make and Protect What's Yours!

For over three decades, Bruce Willey has been educating, entertaining, motivating and inspiring business owners and entrepreneurs to build and grow their businesses with the strategies of his tax planning.

His style inspires and empowers audiences while giving them the tools and strategies they need and want to build and grow successful sustainable brands and businesses.

For more info and to book Bruce for your next event, radio or TV interview, visit: www.brucewilley.com **OR** call +1 (319) 390-5555

One Last, Last Thing...

If you enjoyed this book or found it useful, I'd be very grateful if you'd post a short review on Amazon. Your support really does make a difference. I read all the reviews personally, so I can get your feedback and make this book even better.

If you'd like to leave a review, then all you need to do is click the review link on this book's page on Amazon here:

http://bit.ly/TheSecretSystemUnlocked

Thanks again for your support!

Made in the USA
Middletown, DE
19 September 2019